SPORTS THROUGHOUT HISTORY™

The History of

BASKETBALL

Diana Star Helmer and Thomas S. Owens

The Rosen Publishing Group's
PowerKids Press™
New York

Published in 2000 by The Rosen Publishing Group, Inc.
29 East 21st Street, New York, NY 10010

First Edition

Book Design: Michael de Guzman

Photo Credits: pp. 4, 8 © Naismith Memorial Basketball Hall of Fame; p. 7 CORBIS/Underwood and Underwood; p. 11 © Sportschrome; pp. 12, 16, 19, 20 © AP/Wide World Photos; p. 14 © Jeff Carlick, Rick Kane, Brian Drake/Sportschrome.

Helmer, Diana Star, 1962-
    The history of basketball / by Diana Star Helmer and Thomas S. Owens.
       p.   cm.— (Sports throughout history)
    Includes index.
    Summary: Relates the history of basketball from the 1890s to today, including discussion of prominent teams, women's teams, and the National Basketball Association.
    ISBN 0-8239-5470-6 (lib. bdg. : alk. paper)
    1. Basketball—United States—History—Juvenile literature. [1. Basketball—History.] I. Owens, Tom, 1960- . II. Title. III. Series: Helmer, Diana Star, 1962- Sports throughout history.
GV885.1.H445 1999
796.323'0973—dc21
                                                   99-12140
                                                 CIP

Manufactured in the United States of America

Contents

An Inside Game

In Massachusetts, the winter of 1891 was too cold for outdoor games. Dr. James Naismith, a gym teacher, decided to invent a game his students could play indoors.

The new game was played with a soccer ball, but kicking wasn't allowed. Players had to throw, catch, and jump. They scored points by throwing the ball into a peach basket that Dr. Naismith had asked the janitor to nail on the **balcony** of the gym. The basket was ten feet off the ground. Basketball was born.

◀ *This is Dr. James Naismith and his wife, with the peach baskets that were used in the first basketball games and an early basketball that was invented by a wheelmaker in 1894.*

Basketball Travels

There was no radio or television in 1891. People learned about basketball by seeing or playing it. Men who played basketball taught it to others. The first women's game took place in 1892 at the Springfield, Massachusetts, YMCA, where Dr. Naismith had invented basketball. Word of this new game spread quickly. Teachers in schools and in YMCAs around the country taught the game to their students. By 1895, people all across the U.S. were playing basketball.

From its beginnings, basketball was as popular with women as it was with men. ▶

Putting Up Fences

   Naismith had eighteen students when he invented basketball, so his teams had nine players. Teams were many different sizes until 1896, when two colleges held the first official game with five players on each team.

   There was often a fence around the gym floor. This was because players kept diving into the **bleachers** to get **out-of-bounds** balls. Fans had been hurt. The fence kept wild balls, and players, on the **court**.

◄ *The backboard was invented in 1896 to keep fans in the stands from reaching over and hitting balls out of the basket.*

The Money Game

In 1896, the YMCA team in Trenton, New Jersey, planned a game with a Brooklyn team. Their gym was busy, so the teams decided to rent a gym somwhere else. They sold game tickets to raise money to pay for the other gym. When some money was left over, the players split it. They became basketball's first **professionals**.

Early professional teams were called **barnstormers**. They played local teams, then shared the money from the ticket sales.

The name barnstormers came from actors who performed in barns for money. Basketball players today often make millions of dollars. ▶

The Harlem Globetrotters play ball with the actress Goldie Hawn.

Playing for Fun

When the Harlem Globetrotters started in 1927, most teams were **segregated**. Teams had all black players or all white players. The first Globetrotters were black players who wanted basketball to bring people together. They mixed funny tricks and fancy moves into their games, to show that having fun was more important than winning **championships**. They still travel around the world today, dancing and spinning the ball as they play.

The NBA

The National Basketball Association was formed in 1949. Although early leagues were segregated, African American players have been a part of the NBA almost since it began. Chuck Cooper, the first black NBA player, joined the Boston Celtics in 1950.

"Magic" Johnson, of the L.A. Lakers.

14

Michael Jordan, of the Chicago Bulls. ▶

In the 1980s, basketball became more popular than it had ever been before. Fans loved stars like Julius Erving ("Dr. J."), Larry Bird, Earvin ("Magic") Johnson, and Michael Jordan. These players helped make basketball the well-loved sport it is today.

"Dr. J.," of the Philadelphia 76ers.

◀ *Larry Bird, of the Boston Celtics.*

24
SECOND
SHOT
CLOCK

New Rules

Early basketball **leagues** did not have as many fans as they do today. People thought basketball was boring. Players could dribble and pass the ball as long as they wanted without shooting. This meant that teams didn't make baskets very often. When new rules made the game more exciting, basketball gained popularity. One of the best rules was made by the NBA in 1954. It gives teams just 24 seconds to shoot the ball. That helps make games go by faster.

◀ *Bill Russell of the Boston Celtics lays it up to beat the 24-second shot clock.*

Around the World

   YMCA teachers were the first to take basketball to other countries. Basketball was an **exhibition** sport at the 1904 Olympics. Women in the Soviet Union held their first organized games in 1923. People in China fell in love with basketball soon after that. It became an official Olympic event for men in 1936 and for women in 1976. There are professional leagues in countries like England, Canada, Germany, Greece, Italy, Spain, Yugoslavia, Israel, China, and the Philippines.

Magic Johnson celebrates the U.S. team's gold medal at the 1992 Barcelona Olympics. ▶

When the U.S. team won the 1996 Olympics, more people got excited about women's basketball.

Women's Work

Until recently, American women who wanted to play basketball played in college or in **industrial leagues**. There were no professional women's leagues in the United States that lasted. Talented women who wanted to play basketball professionally had to go overseas. When the U.S. women's team won a gold medal in the 1996 Olympics, the NBA decided to start the Women's National Basketball Association. Today, many American women have the chance to make a living doing what they love: playing basketball.

for Love or Money?

In 1997, when NBA team owners asked their top stars to take less money, the stars refused. Many 1998 games were canceled. Fans were disappointed, but basketball is more than the professional teams. Basketball is kids shooting hoops in driveways and on playgrounds. True basketball fans will always love the game.

Web Sites:

Check out this Web site on basketball: http://www.nba.com

Glossary

balcony (BAL-kuh-nee) An upper floor that sticks out part way over another floor.

barnstormer (BARN-stor-mur) A player on a team that traveled around the country and didn't belong to a league.

bleacher (BLEE-chur) A section of benches at a sports game.

championship (CHAM-pee-un-ship) The last game of a season that decides which team is the best.

court (KORT) The floor where basketball is played.

exhibition (ek-suh-BIH-shun) A game that is just for fun.

industrial league (in-DUS-tree-ul LEEG) Teams made up of people who work together at the same business.

league (LEEG) A group of teams that play against each other in the same sport.

out-of-bounds (OWT-UV-BOWNDZ) When the ball or a player goes off the court.

professional (pruh-FEH-shuh-nul) An athlete who earns money for playing a sport.

segregate (SEH-gruh-gayt) To separate people of different races.

Index